The SPIRITS of '76

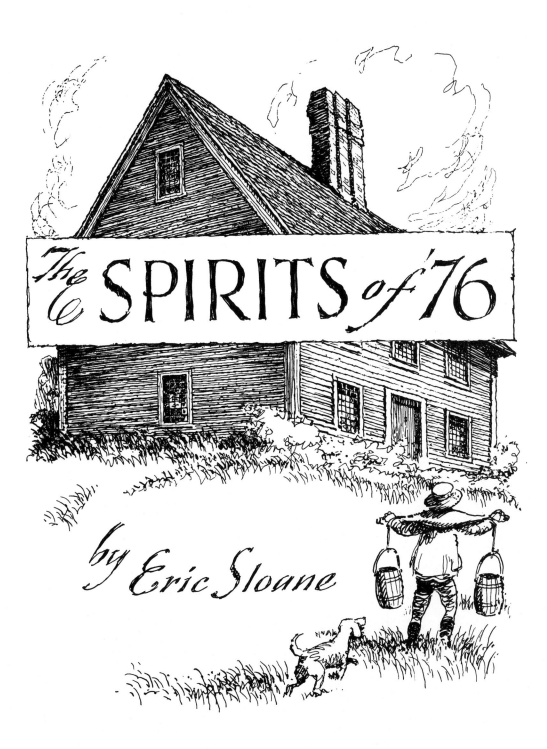

The SPIRITS of '76

by Eric Sloane

BALLANTINE BOOKS · NEW YORK

To
MIMI
who has become
an American citizen
with an abundance
of the original spirits.

BALLANTINE BOOKS
A Division of Random House, Inc.
201 East 50th Street, New York, N.Y. 10022
Simultaneously published by
Ballantine Books of Canada. Ltd., Toronto, Canada

Declaration of Self-Dependence

One night, while reading about the Declaration of Independence, I dozed off wondering what it must have been like to have taken part in its writing. Suddenly I was there. With a quill pen I was writing the great words, "When in the course of human events . . . ." The rest I do not recall, but I remember the title being different—Declaration of Self-Dependence.

As I think now of my dream, the title made more and more sense. The 1776 proclamation referred so much to the American revolutionists that it lacked the flavor of a personal statement. Now, two centuries later, the population and its government have become so vast and complicated that the voice of the individual is vague, weak, and less heard. Perhaps a more pertinent, personal declaration *is* in order, and herewith I present my declaration for today.

When in the course of human events, the material well-being of a society obscures the spiritual principles upon which that society was founded, it becomes proper to review our heritage and redeclare its reason for being. Only by such recollection can a true renaissance of the original American spirit occur.

My nation was born with a declaration of independence, but to be free, I must also practice an *individual* independence.

The statement of 1776 had unique worth because it was the first government manifesto to totally respect the independence of the individual. Different from other national statements of purpose, it was not a declaration of domination but one of liberation.

I hold these truths to be self-evident, that within our democracy the exact principles which rule the conscience and economy of the individual must also govern the conscience and economy of the government. I hold therefore that government waste in any form is intolerable, because just as no family can for long spend more than it earns, neither can a government do so. As frugality is part of the family economy, so must thrift be important to national revenue. The practice of thrift is insurance against greed, which had no part in the original American philosophy.

I hold that respect is the root of morality and that disrespect for oneself, for others, or for the nation is contrary to the American spirit.

I believe that self-dependence produces self-respect. Therefore, helping a man to be self-dependent is an admirable pursuit. But helping a man while taking away his initiative and independence is degrading. Permanently doing for a man what he can do for himself is contrary and destructive to the American tradition. I believe in the dignity of labor and the pursuit of excellence. Therefore, I believe that striving for the most pay for the least amount of work is an immoral aim. It is a principle that cannot endure without eventual demoralization of the worker and decay of workmanship.

Just as you cannot strengthen the weak by weakening the strong, I believe that the wage earner cannot profit by destroying the wage payer. Both capital and labor have equal rights in the American system, and the independence of both is equally deserving of recognition. For either to strike against public welfare or violate the innocent is immoral and against the American tradition.

I believe that the moral strength of the nation is only as strong as the moral strength of its individuals. I therefore commit myself to the pursuit of labor, respect, independence, thrift, excellence, and peace. I hold that self-dependence of the individual is a reflection of self-dependence of the nation, that the American heritage is not only something bestowed upon the individual but, equally, what the individual contributes to his country.

I consider "In God We Trust" a profound statement of national commitment. I believe that democracy without commitment to God is a departure from the original American concept.

I believe that all men are endowed by their Creator with inalienable rights and that the foregoing creed renders not only independence to the nation but self-dependence for each American.

Foreword
200 years of progress ...

It has been said that the worst thing that ever happened to writing was when it became a business. I thought about this when my editor, not long ago, suggested that I consider writing a book for the occasion of the bicentennial of the United States of America. The thought of writing with the incentive of selling, along with the fear that I might add to an inevitable conglomeration of pseudo-patriotic merchandise for 1976 was not at all inspiring. "I'd rather not," I said.

"At least do think about it," he replied.

Perhaps I should not have thought about it for, God help me, an idea was born. It struck me that with the American people preparing to recapture the "spirit of '76" and eager to become immersed in a nostalgic recognition of their past, we should become aware of what the American was two hundred years ago and what we are now. There is a difference and the difference is interesting. The more I thought about this hitherto unconsidered aspect of Americana, the more valuable the idea seemed. Even a reason for a book.

For some years I had researched the physical difference between the early American and his present day counterpart, but I had never thought about any moral or spiritual differences. It began when I viewed a display of death masks of early presidents and great Americans of the eighteenth century and was struck with a certain tininess of features and unusually small-size heads. One of my hobbies had been collecting ancient hats, and although men used to wear their hair full and long, I had never found a hat that would fit my own head. Women's clothing, too, in spite of so many undergarments, was also tiny.

The vision of huge whaling men was shattered when I visited the whaling ship at Mystic, Connecticut, and saw the unbelievably small bunks that they slept in.

Although people were generally smaller, I found that they were wiry and much stronger. Their hearing was more acute and their vision was sharper. Much night work was done without the electric illumination necessary today, and such work as droving and haying and building—even hunting—was done at night and without lights. We must presume their night vision was extraordinary.

We seldom see ourselves growing older. The slow change is insidious and although we are told that time flies, it is hard to realize that it is we who do the flying while time actually stands still: the past is but a moment ago. As I look into the mirror, I seem to believe that I always had these wrinkles and that my hair was always this gray, and if a boyish face appeared, it would be more shock than pleasure. It is the same with a nation: we tend to believe that we are exactly like the early American but wiser and much more experienced—that today is no more than a yesterday grown older. We have learned to accept the fact that the horse and buggy is gone forever, but it is hard to realize that the man who drove that horse and buggy is gone, too.

The truth is that 1776 belongs to 1776. We cannot hope to recapture the old ways easily, partly because we have so destroyed our past but also because we ourselves have become different. The godly, frugal, content, thankful, work-loving man of yesterday has now become the money-oriented, extravagant, discontented, thankless, work-shunning man of today. The original spirits of America past have become worn out, obsolete, and not very adaptable to modern living.

It might be enlightening, I thought, to delve into this theory, to isolate some of these "vanishing spirits," and parade them before a reading audience. It could possibly revive some of the valuable philosophies of early times that should not have become lost; perhaps some of the valuable original American spirits could be rekindled.

Man so often comments: "If we only knew then what we know now," but few of us consider: "If we only could know *now* what they knew *then!*" History does a good job of recording what man *does*, yet so seldom has it recorded the way man *thought*. The modern American boasts of having "know how" but the old-timers had something we have lost along the way—the American "*know-why.*"

I believe the greatest change in American thinking occurred in the middle 1800s; Abraham Lincoln sensed this and he was duly alarmed. "Our progress in degeneracy," he said, "appears to be pretty rapid." He then spelled out the trend of change in a thought-provoking paragraph remarkably pertinent to our present time:

> You cannot bring about prosperity by discouraging thrift. You cannot strengthen the weak by weakening the strong. You cannot help the wage earner by pulling down the wage payer. You cannot help the poor by destroying the rich. You cannot build character and courage by taking away a man's initiative and independence. You cannot help men permanently by doing for them what they could and should do for themselves.

Lincoln had a profound understanding and respect for the American dream. Overcome with emotion in Independence Hall, he made an impromptu and little known speech:

"I have often pondered over the dangers which were incurred by the men who assembled here to frame and adopt that Declaration.... I have often inquired of myself what great principle or idea it was that kept this Confederacy together since. It was not the mere separation of the colonies from the motherland, but that sentiment in the Declaration of Independence which gave liberty, not alone to the people of this country, but hope to all the world for all future time; that the weight would be lifted from the shoulders of all men and that all would have an equal chance. Now my friends, can this country be saved on that basis? If it can, I will consider myself one of the happiest men in the world if I can help save it. . . . but if this country cannot be saved without giving up that principle, I would rather be assassinated on this spot rather than surrender it."

I suppose growing philosophical is not in keeping with the popular gay spirit of celebration but a two hundredth birthday seems to deserve at least some solemn memorialization. Our yearly firecracker Fourth of July commemorated by very confused millions has lost too much of its original profundity: perhaps a bicentennial *thoughtfulness* could revive something of that first Independence Day celebrated by a very dedicated few.

We charm ourselves into believing that we have a birthday each year: the truth is that there is only one birthday; all the others are merely celebrations of that past event. Stopping long enough to glance backward to see where we once were and where we are now can be enlightening, possibly critical.

Some of the world's greatest minds have in the last few years agreed with ecologists that at the rate man is proceeding, another century could very well mark the beginning of the end of all civilization: the increasing air and water and land pollution certainly indicates this statement to be possible (although such chaos can be halted or at least slowed down). The pollution of spirit is with us, too, and at the rate we are going, the next hundred years can have done drastic things to the human spirit as well; yet chaos of the *spirit* can be halted or slowed down, too.

The first United States centennial in 1876 was mostly a display of inventions. Instead of commemorating the American spirit there were vast halls of new machinery and exhibits of scientific progress: I wonder, now, how many of those inventions have provided us in the past century with more means for cultural deterioration and less reason for mankind to think. William Morris's comment on the 1876 centennial was that: "the great achievement of the nineteenth century were its wonders of invention, skill and patience which were used for the production of measureless quantities of worthless make-shifts."

Albert Schweitzer said, "Man has lost the capacity to foresee and to forestall: he will end by destroying the earth." Actually nothing is taken from nor added to the earth and man simply rearranges, pollutes or wastes its resources; so man cannot "destroy the earth" although he *can* destroy it for his own use, and so eventually destroy himself. The corporate life may appear prosperous and healthy in spite

10

of the presence of spiritual cancer: although we tend to believe our existence depends upon science and invention, the real soul of man is *spirit*.

Thomas Edison, when told that he had contributed more to civilization than any other human being, said: "Civilization doesn't really lean on inventions: the most necessary task of civilization is to teach man to *think*." I hope that after two centuries of scientific progress, we can finally afford to mark time long enough and let spiritual progress catch up with it. Herewith I have considered ten early American spirits, which I believe have either weakened or vanished. The reader might disagree with me; on the other hand he might add a few to my list. In either case, we both will have done some important thinking and my book will then have been worthwhile.

Eric Sloane
Warren, Connecticut

Some of the many flags respected by the Early American.

DONT TREAD ON ME

Washington's Grand Union

The Spirit of RESPECT

F or so young a nation there is an amazing amount of accepted misinformation about the history of the United States of America. One of the more well-known patriotic paintings is that of George Washington crossing the Delaware, standing up in a twelve-foot rowboat (with twelve others!) carrying Old Glory, which was a flag yet to be born. The flag George carried, if ever, was called the Grand Union, which was the British Union Jack upon the Merchant Marine stripes. But in the beginning there were more than a dozen versions of the American emblem and almost as many versions of respect to the national flag.

I have often quipped that the best way to learn any subject is to write a book about it, and researching early American patriotism was no exception. When I began compiling my group of vanishing spirits with patriotism at the head of my list, I at once began learning. With frequent flag-burnings, with the stars and stripes being worn on the backsides of blue jeans and the Pledge of Allegiance ruled out as unconstitutional, I presumed that American patriotism must be at an all-time low, and that it was the national spirit most in need of return. As I researched and analyzed the subject, however, I soon realized that patriotism has become all too closely related with war: the most patriotic people in history (like the Nazis) were always the most warlike and ruthless. Great thinkers, I learned, very often frown upon patriotism, and the more I thought about this spirit, the more I too wondered about its real values. "This heroism upon command," wrote Einstein, "this senseless violence, this accursed bombast of *patriotism* —how intensely do I despise it!" One philosopher called patriotism "the religion of Hell."

I had never regarded patriotism in such a light and I began to think. I remembered my first encounter with pseudopatriotism about half a century ago while I was a student at military academy: while folding the flag at sundown with a fellow student, I had accidently let it fall to the ground. "You son of a bitch!" my helper cried. "You let the American flag touch the ground!"

That was long ago when obscenities were treated as obscenities and I wasn't going to allow anyone to call my mother a dog. A fist fight followed and I still carry a small scar of the incident. I suppose it was a mini example of how wars start, where there is as much punishment to the punisher as there is to the sufferer, all in the name of patriotism.

Stephen Decatur's "Our country right or wrong" had often worried me; I found more to my liking, Carl Schurz's "Our Country right or wrong—*when right to be kept right and when wrong to be put right.*" And so I wondered if we have not been using the word incorrectly (or even the wrong word). I went to my collection of ancient dictionaries. In one old volume such as might have been used by George Washington or Nathan Hale or Patrick Henry and other early patriots, I found the answer: we certainly have been using the word incorrectly.

Patriotism in the old sense was defined as "The Spirit of acting like a Father to one's country: a Publick Spiritedness." This definition is quite different from today's: "One who guards his country's welfare, especially a defender of popular liberty." I recalled how Hitler described Nazism as "the popular liberty" and his storm troopers were known as "defenders of popular liberty." War, I realized, has for a long while been waged in the name of *patriotism* instead of *nationalism*. Nationalism has been one of the most killing diseases of mankind. The American Revolution was actually a patriotic revolution *against* *nationalism*.

The difference between twentieth century *patriotism* and eighteenth century *respect* became more evident as I researched. Johnson said, "Patriotism is the last refuge of a scoundrel" and Russell said, "Patriotism is the willingness to kill and be killed for trivial reasons." Perry said, "Patriotic fervor can obliterate moral distinctions altogether." But Washington used Shakespeare's words: "I do love my country's good with a *respect* more tender, more holy and profound than mine own life. "After what I owe to God, nothing should be more sacred than the respect I owe to my country." I began to realize that the early patriot was more aware of his national position than the present day patriot.

I suppose the first great American patriots were those fifty-six men who signed their names to their own death warrant on July fourth in 1776. Yet their names are nearly forgotten to history: the average American can name only three or four of the signers of that profound declaration. One librarian was embarrassed about not being able to recall any others "besides George Washington and Patrick Henry": of course, neither on had signed. Soon forgotten, true patriotism is a very personal emotion, asking no reward.

Looking away from the battlefields for an example of patriotism is difficult at first; but they do happen all around us and every day. I found one such example at a wedding anniversary dinner. I don't like country club affairs and so I really had not looked forward to Haig Tashjian's surprise party. Other than my wife and myself, all were Armenian. A diminutive lady arose during the dinner and made a toast. She confided that she was nearing one hundred years of age and she told how her family had fled in fear of the Turks, and how she came to America. Then she told how America had fulfilled its promises of being a good home for Armenians just as it has for so many other European people. "And so my toast," she said, "is not only to the wedded couple, but to the country that has made everything possible for them and for us. Before I sit down, I want to lead you all in singing 'God Bless America'."

As the chorus ended I could hear the faraway strains of a rock-and-roll band playing in some adjoining banquet room; there was a meaningful hush as many wiped away a tear; then the dinner continued. I felt unusually proud to be a native American, and thankful to Armenia for fathering such a gracious people. I had witnessed the inspiration of true patriotism, heroism in humility. Peace has just as worthy patriots as the battlefield.

In the beginning, the word *patriotism* came from the word *pater* (father) and patriotism was "a quality of respect of one who is devoted to his *family* in a fatherly fashion"; it had little to do with war or nationalism. Therefore, I offer that the word *patriotism* be substituted whenever possible, by the better word *respect*. I find respect to be the vanishing American spirit most worthy of return to our beloved nation.

Respect for family, respect for the nation and the land, respect for the flag and the law, respect for mankind and respect for oneself —these have been outstandingly wanting during the last few years. Within the family, within the nation and to all other nations, the only hope for the survival of civilization is respect or love for one another. In the end, this is all that matters.

Native Americans are so frequently disrespectful to their nation that it comes as a pleasing and heartening surprise to witness respect for us from those born elsewhere. The attendant where the Liberty Bell was shown found it interesting that those who most often removed their hats as they beheld the great bell were foreigners. Once two blind Japanese soldiers in uniform came "to see" the bell, and asked the attendant to read to them the inscription thereon. He led their hands over the raised letters and he showed them where the crack was. He watched them leave, talking excitedly in their own language and he wondered exactly what their reaction had been. But stuffed into the bell's crack, he found two roses that the veterans had been wearing. "I didn't think Japanese soldiers could have done it to me," he said, "but at that instant I had even more love for America, and respect for the old bell, than ever before."

Adlai Stevenson seldom used the word patriotism. "When an American says he loves his country, he doesn't refer to the purple mountain majesties and amber waves of grain. Instead he means that he loves an inner air, an inner light in which freedom lives and in which a man can draw the breath of self-*respect*."

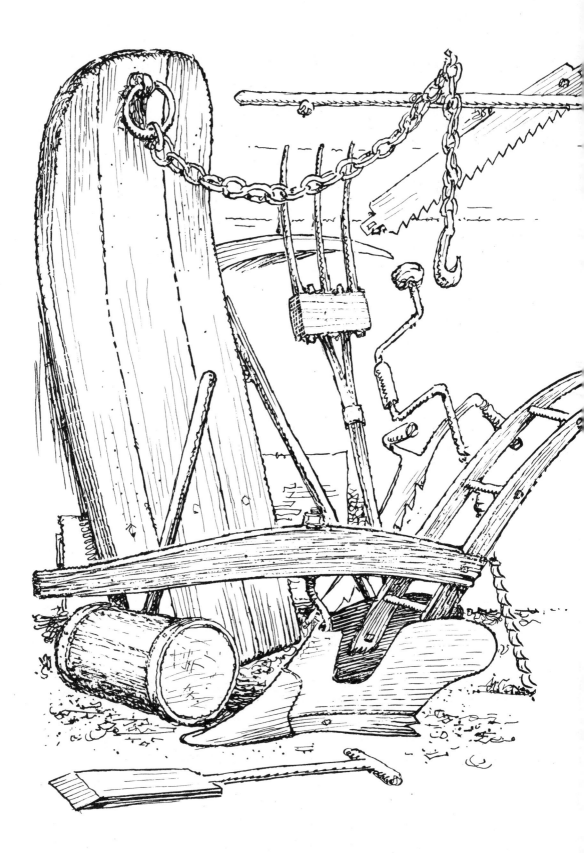

The Spirit of Hard WORK

I gathered together a museum of early American tools partly because of their historical value and also because their design made them works of art hard to resist collection. But those who come to view them now seem mostly impressed by their size and weight: the tools of the pioneers seem to have been designed for giants. Axes that are difficult to lift, let alone swing by the hour; stone boats weighing hundreds of pounds; fifty-pound sledge hammers; planes and chisels three times larger than the ones we use today. "They make me exhausted just looking at them," said one visitor. "Those men must have been gluttons for punishment." Those men, believe it or not, did not regard work as punishment; they found a dignity in sweat.

One of the oldest diaries in my collection reads: "October 20. (1760) Celebrated the reward of the cleared north field." For a long while I presumed there might have found a sum of money in the field, until I contemplated a sampler that came with my farmhouse, which was obviously sewn by a young girl: "See only that thou work hard and thou canst not escape the reward." It is significant of our times that we often associate the word *reward* with *cash;* the reward of happiness used to lie less in the possession of money and more in the joy of achievement. When a New England field was cleared of stones and stumps, I have since learned, the occasion was celebrated with a feast called a "reward dinner."

Once upon a time in America, hard work was a part of life; it was one of the pleasures and satisfactions of living. Even as I write these words they have a ridiculous ring to my ear, so conditioned am I to the popular American creed of seeking the most pay for the least amount of work. Hard labor is considered either drudgery or punishment or, at best, a necessary evil; and the man who works harder than his fellow worker nowadays is considered not only foolish but a danger to the economy. He is even liable for reprimand or penalty by his union management.

Retirement from labor has become a national aim, and the physical and mental pleasure from hard work has become a vanished American spirit. Here and there where excellence is involved, foreign economies have undermined our capitalistic economy, and I wonder how often a difference in the national spirit of labor could be involved. Retirement elsewhere is a personal decision, but in American business it is a sudden blow, often at the time of a man's life when his talents are at a peak.

As I sit in my studio and look out over the New England landscape laced together by ribbons of stone fencing, I wonder at the long man hours and unbelievable strength, often of old men, that must have gone into the clearing of such virgin land two centuries ago. The greater wonder, however, is that these people so enjoyed their work that they were thereby more aware of the meaning of life and that they were actually more satisfied beings than we are today.

Robb Golding was one of the last of that vanishing race of old-time Maine guides. "He is an old friend," my wife said, "and he is coming this spring to prepare a garden for us." One day in May, Robb arrived and the next morning during breakfast I began to wonder at what time one should awaken a ninety-two-year-old man.

At that moment he appeared at the kitchen door. "I hope I didn't waken you," he said in his Maine accent. "Sure enough tried to be quiet but I kept striking your confounded Connecticut stones.

Most times I rise at four thirty but I overslept a mite this time. Didn't start work till six!''

At the end of two days, Robb had laid out an extraordinary garden with a split rail fence around it. I suppose local help would have made it a week's work. "How much are we going to pay him?'' I asked my wife. "Good Lord!'' she exclaimed. "Don't mention pay to him. He has more money than we have and besides it would hurt his feelings.'' Then she told me how Robb makes a trip each spring to make gardens for his good friends; how he enjoyed working in the earth and how planting gave him the feeling of having done something to repay his Maker for the spirit of life. With dimmed vision and nearly deaf, he could prepare a garden exactly as he did nearly three-quarters of a century ago, which gave him a profound satisfaction and a reason for living.

I did manage to bring up the subject of pay however, and Robb gave me a lesson in human nature. "Work is work when you're paid to do it,'' he said. "When you do it without pay, it becomes your pleasure. There's a lot of time in heaven for me to rest, so I want to get in all the working hours I can while I'm still alive.'' I asked him if that didn't tire him. "It sure does,'' he said. "But that's a good feeling.'' Fatigue, I suppose, is a splendid pillow.

At ninety-three, Robb had finished a garden for a friend in New York State, and the mattress of freshly turned turf in the shade of an apple tree in blossom was too much of a temptation: he stretched out on the ground to rest. He had closed his eyes for the last time and it was a good way for a man to leave this earth. Especially for Robb.

Recently I went to the midwest to bring back a ton of my paintings, which had been the feature of a State Fair. I don't usually regard my work by the pound, but the end-of-summer heat, the smells and sounds of carnival activities just at closing time, plus the prospect of my long trip home, created a definite and depressing weight to the drab occasion; I felt surrounded by a completely uninspiring world. A morning walk through the city only added to my melancholy. A shoe-shine shop just opening for the day's business seemed a likely place to rest and contemplate. An aged black man started to brush my shoes.

A strange thing then occurred, for my shoe-shine became a starting performance. Three times the old fellow left and returned with half empty bottles of cleaning liquids with which he removed all of the previous polish. He picked away tiny specks of paint with his fingernails, and with the heel of his hand he applied new wax with reverent strokes. "I hope you are not in a hurry," he said. After what seemed more than a half hour, he spat lightly on what looked like a new pair of shoes and then produced a chamois for a final gloss. I had witnessed an artist at work. "Thank you for being so patient," he said. "I like to do a perfect job."

When he saw the bill I gave him, he said: "I can't get change for that so early in the morning." But somehow I had forgotten my dreariness: the world and mankind miraculously seemed more promising. "That's not pay," I told him. "That is a gift from one artist to another." What connection there is between painting and shoe-shining is obscure, but to me it was real. Artistry is stimulating and contagious, and I knew from that small performance, my own work would benefit.

For about a century in America, people created beautiful gardens and made their homes and furniture, raised flax and wool and cloth to make their own clothes. Everyone was his own craftsman and it was an age when individualism flourished. Then Ralph Waldo Emerson, who should have said: "Make a *good* mousetrap and the world will beat a path to your door," instead said: "Make a *better* mousetrap." Individualism met head-on with something called competition.

Until that time, according to the old dictionaries, competition meant "endeavoring to gain what another is endeavoring to gain at the same time; common strife; rivalry. Complete competition," the dictionary continued, "occurs in war." It was a dirty word then, but now as business battles the good war of competition, the lonely individual lives in his twilight of self-expression.

Both business and war establishments will argue that scientific progress is largely the result of competitiveness. The truth is that both business and war efforts do spur scientific progress and make use of the inventor, but the inventor himself is neither businessman nor warrior. The inventor is an individualist and seldom a competitor. Nothing worthwhile in civilization has ever been created by competition alone: no great doctor, educator, inventor, scientist, writer, or artist became successful trying to compete with another doctor, educator, inventor, scientist, writer, or artist. Christ was not a competitor. Great deeds are born from within—not in a race to win or to overpower someone else.

In today's world almost everything is done for us; we are

deprived of that satisfaction of creation and accomplishment. The greatest reward of a thing well done is to have done it all yourself. Thoreau said the prime aim of the laborer should be not to make his living but to perform a certain work well. "Do not hire a man who does your work for money," he said, "but him who does it for love of it."

I have a friend who, with the fortune of an overwhelming inheritance, has retired to yachting and golfing. He chose to visit me while I was building the stone wall of my studio, and he offered to spend the time helping me. At the end of a back-breaking day, he confided: "I haven't had such an appetite since I was young, and I've never felt better. Boy, am I going to sleep tonight!" He had forgotten how good it feels to be hungry and tired. "What you are enjoying," I told him, "is the rare satisfaction of hard labor!" I suppose if I sailed or golfed with the same enthusiasm with which I build stone walls, I might become just as hungry and tired at the end of each day, but then I wouldn't have a stone wall to crown my feeling of satisfaction. I think I like my own life pattern.

The early American farmer left countless monuments behind, all results of the spirit of hard labor. Their work was often done long after what we now call the age of retirement; if leaving a national heritage behind was considered, they performed well; I am constantly inspired by their efforts. The stone walls flowing into the horizon of my farmland and the massive beams above me in my barn studio are far more than just decorative things; they are stimulating remembrances of a hard-working pioneer America. It makes me think of the motto on the sampler. It has been a long while in America since hard work has been regarded as a pleasure and satisfaction of life, and that if "thou work hard, thou canst not escape the reward."

1976

The Spirit of FRUGALITY

One of the more irksome comments to an antique shop proprietor is the frequent remark, "Look at the price of this thing—my family had one like it and they threw it away!" If great-great grandfather was not a frugal man, of course, there would be very few antique shops today.

Out my way, one of the things to do on a nice day is to visit the town dump. There, for some reason or other, you can often find extraordinary treasures that have been thrown away; old doors, ancient hinges, bottles, hand-hewn beams, and all the things that have been discarded and replaced by something new. The highway department truckmen, who use the dump often, found enough odds and ends to outfit their garage office with good furniture, a heating system, an organ, a kitchen, and parts enough to build both a motorcycle and a farm truck. One workman with a sense of humor made a sign saying: "Beautify your town dump—throw away something beautiful." Even in New York City I have seen furniture and items packed and waiting on the sidewalks for the sanitation truck, things that could sell easily in a show window. City people even abandon their automobiles as cast-off junk, leaving them along the street to be towed away.

Throwing things away has become an American habit. It has been estimated that we waste more in one second than our gross national earning of two hundred years ago. There were no garbage dumps in those days because all leftovers were reused. In fact the word "garbage" in 1776 referred only to tripe and the entrails of cattle. There was no such thing as junk yards because nothing was ever cast away, and the word "junk" in 1776 referred to short lengths of rope. Both garbage and junk, major problems now, were unheard of then.

It must have made life powerfully meaningful and extraordinarily exciting to create necessities like soap and candles and gunpowder and clothing and shoes and medicine all from simple leftovers. Table scraps and meat fat miraculously became scented soap; the barnyard yielded the makings of gunpowder; old plaster and cow dung became fertilizer for the garden; most of the wrought iron tools around the farm were recreated from other broken or discarded implements.

In my own lifetime I recall people saving tinfoil and balls of string. My father's cellar had cans of assorted nails and screws and objects that always seemed to find a place in his life years later. It stretches the imagination now, but frugality was once an American trait.

The spirit of frugality began its decline slowly until the last few decades of acceleration, when we have overcome the fine art of saving and finally established a unique economy of waste. The government seems to have proven to us that the more it spends of our money, the richer we become. Of course a nation is no more than a group of individuals, and what applies to the group should also apply to the individual, but this age defies logic.

When America was new, its economy was based upon the management of the individual household. In fact the word economy (from the Greek for "house management") referred to the business of house-keeping, and an "economist" was simply a good housekeeper.

"Any government, like any family," said F. D. Roosevelt, "can occasionally spend a little more than it earns. But you and I know that continuance of that habit means the poor-house." It is obvious that if any American family operated its finances by the same logic as their government, the family would become bankrupt quickly. Economy, whether public or private, cannot tolerate waste, and to base an economy upon waste is insanity.

Frugality is frowned upon as being associated with stinginess or poverty, yet it is actually a source of the richer life because frugality is founded on the principle that all wealth has limits. Frugality is also a mark of intelligence and sensitivity: the artist or writer knows the value of being frugal with his brush strokes or with his words; he knows how extravagance usually produces little other than bad taste.

I recall buying an oval rag rug from an aged Connecticut farm-wife. Tears came to her eyes as she contemplated the rug and its sale. "I started that center part," she said, "when we first started farming; you can still see the dyed flour sacks we used for curtains. Then farther on there's some blue gingham—that's from the first dress Bob bought me . . . and even a bit of the baby's pink crib cover!" The continuous cord of rag material, probably a quarter of a mile long, spelled out a large piece of her life, all made from rags such as most people throw away. She had saved a lot of memories. "I'll come back another time," I lied to her, "when I have the cash with me." Of course, I didn't return.

A recent auction of "a farmhouse and contents" in Connecticut brought fair prices for the modern kitchen and dining room items, a little more for the old bedroom pieces, but the attic produced articles of incredible value. "They probably didn't know what they were storing," said the auctioneer, "but the simple stuff they had saved for years brought in more money than the whole house and all the land!"

If Christ were here today and He were given a gift of a million dollars, I do not think He would buy stock with it. Yet if you confront anyone with the question of what he would do with a million dollars, even a child will come up with the prompt reply that he would "invest it wisely." In other words, even though he had received an amount he might have worked a lifetime to amass, he would still be most concerned with making that into an even *larger* amount. Very few would think of bestowing the whole gift to a charitable cause.

"Savings" nowadays refers only to *money;* if you say a person "saves" a lot, you usually infer that he has a lot of cash to show for it. Two hundred years ago, however, money did not have the importance it has now: it was even considered rude to include money in your conversation. I have a collection of early newspapers advertising houses and land and all sorts of merchandise, yet there is never mention of any price! I also have an early collection of wills, and I seldom find any mention of money. Today a rich man's will involves mostly cash holdings, but the old-timer's savings were in his woodpile, his rootcellar, his silo and bank barns, his haystacks, manure, livestock, carriages, buldings and land. "Money," said Thoreau, "is not necessary to buy one's necessities of the soul."

The old-timer kept his cash assets either in a sugar bowl or in his back pocket. He collected pieces of his own life and labors but he seldom collected money. Among my antiques is the inventory of the estate of the man who in 1745 owned my farm and built the house and barn upon it. When business is slow, and I begin to feel sorry for myself, I mix a drink, make a good fire in my fireplace, and read that ancient paper. After listing the old man's clothing and his household furniture, there is mention of *four gold coins;* then there is "1 Bible, 1 geography, 1 Rules of Life, 1 woman's saddle, 1 cow, 1 shoe-making set, 1 looking glass, 1 wash tub and two churns, 1 tin stove, 2 axes, 2 mares, 2 bedsteads and hooks, 1 pewter teapot." This amounted to about two hundred dollars' worth of material assets but I am sure he was a richer man than I, but as I contemplate his life and holdings, I realize how fortunate am I.

Unless in extreme poverty, it seems strange that anyone's personal effects could be so limited; yet to the early farmer it would seem more strange that any sane person would buy something he didn't need. Today, nearly half of the national spending is for things not actually needed. The things we thought were needed, that which did not last as long as it should, things that failed to do the proper job, and things accepted as waste, account for some extravagance, but military waste is so enormous as to be beyond valuation or comprehension.

One of my farming friends once remarked that "there are a lot of people living within their means, and that sort of thing is ruining the economy." I suppose *saving* is an unhealthy word in Washington, but I would enjoy seeing some of Franklin's sayings about frugality on such buildings as the Pentagon. Perhaps his adage: "Make no expense but that it do good to others or yourself—i.e., waste nothing." How out of place it would be!

The Spirit of
THANKFULNESS

The spirit of thankfulness in America like the day set aside for its celebration has changed considerably. There are very few records of how our first holidays were spent, so we must rely more on personal diaries rather than on printed history. One early mention involves the Pennsylvania German custom of gathering harvest foods in a basket beneath a fruit tree where the farm family would gather for its private thanksgiving service, a plate set out for each member.

History would have us believe that from the beginning the American thanksgiving was a day of merriment and feasting but the pioneer colonist would have regarded that as pure blasphemy. Like Christmases in those days, the occasion was usually solemn and Puritan, with more fasting than feasting: Actually the first thanksgiving feasts were the ending of thanksgiving *fasts*. In the Puritan code, feasts and fasts kept close company. Up until 1800 the day was primarily a church observance and also a time for family reunion. My earliest dictionary mentions Thanksgiving as: "a Holy Day set aside for religious services; a celebration of divine goodness and mercy."

Thanksgiving and *fast* were mentioned together as late as 1835 when the Connecticut General Assembly repealed a law which: "prohibits service labor and recreation on days of *fast* and *thanksgiving* (subject to a fine of four dollars)." It does seem strange that with so many things to be thankful for now in the United States, our divine gratitude should be so connected with eating.

Once a year for the past half century I am reminded of a certain Thanksgiving Day dinner in a Kansas restaurant. I had run away from home to earn my way about the country as a sign-painter, and my box of paints (which also contained my worldly goods and a clean change of clothing) was always with me: I tucked the box under the table. The restaurant was one of those typical small town places called a cafe, but the word was pronounced like "calf." The meal was memorable. When I had finished and asked for the check, the proprietor gave me a slip of paper with a penciled message. "Happy Thanksgiving," it said. "There is no charge for food on this day. We are only thankful that you came by." I have long forgotten the town and the man's name, but I have carried with me that memory of American graciousness for fifty years.

Another gracious restauranteur was Joseph Sartori, a poor immigrant who started Joe's Restaurant in Coney Island and soon became a rich American. I remember how, when his waiters were in need or were about to have an addition to their family, an unsigned envelope would appear at their home containing cash. Joe had prospered without help from anyone and it became his religion to dispose of his profits anonymously to those who deserved his secret gifts.

But I also remember how Joe went out of business, a sad man. He had fired a waiter whom he had found to be dishonest. The union, however, disagreed with Joe and surrounded his restaurant with chanting pickets. I shall never forget an Italian busboy who marched alongside the pickets with his own handmade sign. It read: MR. SARTORI IS NOT AN UNFAIR MAN. HE IS A GOOD MAN. GOD BLESS HIM. PLEASE EAT AT HIS RESTAURANT. It is easy and popular nowadays to display discontent and complaint, but to voice gratitude is remarkable.

The art of being thankful in America has not progressed in spite of two hundred years of all sorts of amazing things to be thankful for. The gifts of life are more and more taken for granted and the general belief is that we constantly deserve more than whatever we already have. For example, the common response from the recipients of charity (now called relief or welfare) is that the gifts are always too small. Voicing gratitude is out of fashion, rare or unheard of.

Pioneer Americans were rich in the spirit of thankfulness. When the *Mayflower* weighed anchor at Plymouth, the first act of human expression was to gather on deck for prayers; the first steps ashore were followed by kneeling in the sand for another prayer of thanks. It was the proper way of life in those days to be grateful often and to express it openly.

Thankfulness happened to be an important tie to friendship with the American Indians who regarded gratitude above simple good manners: to them, ingratitude was the unpardonable sin and gratitude was godliness: their ceremonies were full of thanksgivings. "We are grateful for the land," goes one common prayer of the Red Man, "and for all the things upon the land which the Spirit has bestowed." In the dust wherever modern progress has buried other cultures, we have buried much of the magic of earlier civilizations.

Although we have progressed technologically to an astounding degree, we have stood still (or often receded) spiritually. I listened recently to a Quaker speak of twentieth-century avarice. "Greed," he said, "has been the downfall of individuals and of nations, too. We constantly expect more than that which we have. We take all that is given us though never really meant for us, and do this without even acknowledging our act to God." The comment seemed timely, but he was actually reading from the writings of an earlier American Quaker named William Penn. It is sad that spiritual progress has not kept stride with technology.

Twentieth-century prayer seems mostly confined to requests, but old-time prayers were more often expressions of thanksgiving. Grace at table was said before and after each meal—first a thanking for the food and then thanks for the enjoyment of having eaten it. An interesting rule at Harvard in 1650 stated: "Neither may any Schollar rise from his place or goe out of ye Hall at mealtime before Thanksgiving bee ended." A rule like that now in the average American school would be regarded as unconstitutional Puritanism, but seventeenth century Harvard regarded it "a simple decency inspired by the Dignity of Man and the general Spirit of the Collidge."

The early farmer practiced grace at the table but it didn't stop there. The phrase "knocking on wood" indicated that moment when he closed the barn for the night and as the latch was put in place, he expressed thankfulness with a ceremonial knock on the wooden door frame. One vanished early American holiday was Plow Monday when farmers began their season of farm work. On this Monday after the Twelfth Day of January, the first farm chore of the year was to attend church; there they gave thanks that last year's bounties had lasted them through the winter. On the first of August when the farming season ended, Lammis Day was another early thanksgiving ceremony; the head of the household went to church in the morning of that day with a loaf of bread made from the year's first grain. This "Lammis Loaf" was consecrated and it became the center of a Lammis Day Feast at noon, very much like our present Thanksgiving Day feast.

The standard American Thanksgiving Day, according to history, originated in 1630 during one of the coldest days in February when foodstores had run low and supplies from England failed to arrive. A meeting was held to declare a time for fasting and prayer; but on that very day a ship appeared and the occasion changed from a fast to a feast. Actually the Indian thanksgiving feast of corn and turkey and pumpkin-squash was observed long before the white man arrived; we really copied an Indian Thanksgiving menu and haven't gone far from it since then.

February 1630, the date of our first national Thanksgiving Day, along with its reason for being, has changed several times. Only two years later—in 1632—it was proclaimed as "a publique thanksgiving day throughout the several plantations, to be observed on June thirteenth." In the South the day was altered to June 28. Then in 1788 the date was changed by Congress to December 30, but George Washington in 1789 changed it to November 26. In 1863 President Lincoln decided it should be the last Thursday in November, and that went well until merchants said it was too close to Christmas. So Franklin Delano Roosevelt agreed that the Thursday before would balance our holidays better, and bargain store sales and overeating in the name of thanksgiving are now established Americana for that date.

No nation to date, has done more for the spirit of man and given him the promise of Independence, than the United States of America; therefore to the generous mind, the debt of gratitude to America is worldwide. If there might be only one expression of celebration commemorating the birth of the Declaration of Independence, it would well be an expression of gratitude.

God grant that the spirit of gratefulness again become a national trait—that in between year-long demonstrations of unrest and complaint, we might be treated to occasional demonstrations of thankfulness.

the Spirit of PIONEERING

Adventure is not outside a man, but within.

Mark Grayson must have been an adventurer at heart. His carpenter shop in Hartford was doing well enough but his longing to travel westward was an obstinate urge. He would wake in the middle of the night from dreaming about Indians and buffalo, beholding a prairie landscape that he was confident he would some day farm.

The cross-country roads in 1850 were what we would now call a path; yet on horseback and leading a farm wagon full of stores for a winding five hundred miles, Mark and his wife managed to reach Pennsylvania where the already famous Conestoga wagons were built. A new wagon and proper equipment left only what cash Mark carried in his pants pocket. The trip from Hartford to Pennsylvania became nearly half a year of continuous hardship, but traveling in the new wagon promised even more strenuous adventure. They headed westward toward wherever the horizon presented the least mountains, and one mile a day was sometimes an accomplishment. Wherever there was a river or even a stream to cross, travel became a remarkable and exciting engineering project.

Mark never did reach the far west for somewhere near where Columbus now stands, the Ohio prairies seemed to offer the exact farmsite he had so often dreamed of. With the help of the government and a railroad grant, fifty acres became the Grayson farm. What Mark and his wife did there is not fully recorded, but there is a shopping center where Mark's cornfield stood and a gas station was built over the foundation of his farmhouse. A bulldozer had considerable trouble moving some of the old stone fences: the operator wondered how anyone a century ago could have piled up half-ton rocks in so precise a manner. "Most likely with a team of oxen." They were last remaining monuments to the strange and wonderful spirit of pioneering that Americans once had—a spirit that could prompt a man to suffer unbelievable hardships across country, to seek out bleak, uninhabited land and, in claiming it as his own, find satisfaction and content and happiness to make it worthwhile.

The spirit of adventure has faded and the pioneers' great-great-grandchildren are not easily persuaded that farming is the honorable calling it used to be. We must face the fact that the splendid story of the American pioneer is finished and that no new story worthy of taking its place has yet begun.

Without adventure, civilization is automatically in the process of decay. Whether scientific venture or business explorations can really take the place of romantic adventure is sad conjecture. You might argue that with electronics and space flight or moon exploration, adventure is really an all-time high today, until we realize that we are now mere watchers instead of participators and that modern society has become an outsider to all pioneering.

It is always heartening to behold how a small child finds adventure in the most commonplace act and we know it is because he is doing something for the first time. Nowadays there are very few first times because everything has already been done for us and life often becomes boring. Turning a thermostat to make heat is an astounding improvement over chopping down a tree, sawing it into kindling and logs, and then building a fire in the fireplace. But the invigoration of exercise in the forest, the smell of pine kindling, the comfortable warmth of flaming oak, and the sight of glowing embers in your own hearth, have become almost vanished Americana. Push-button life is without much adventure. I remember when flying was part of flight, feeling each updraft and downdraft, climbing with it and experiencing the splendid phenomenon of flight: now the feeling of flight is like that of riding in an elevator. Each scientific advance makes life simpler but duller, without adventure.

My own good fortune of living in the country affords me tiny but constant adventures; they are not like those of everyday pioneer life but they do make country living attractive and I become sad for those city people who miss such joys. Even my walk down my own lane to the mailbox each day is an adventure: when the mailman chooses to deliver to my house a package too large to fit the mailbox, I feel deprived of that small experience of the day. Adventure, after all, is as big or as little as you care to make it; Thoreau found it even in plain solitude.

It has always given me wonder why ninety percent of the people choose to live in ten percent of America's landspace, subjecting themselves to the insidious debasement of overcrowding. Out there between cities, in mountains and prairies, are still hundreds of thousands of empty acres of adventure and health and meaningful living, being ignored by both people and government. Abraham Lincoln said: "I am in favor of cutting up the wild lands into parcels, so that every poor man can have a home." It was a good idea then, but man has changed: he doesn't want to own his own living space. Homes are not built for future generations; they house children until they are old enough to leave home. The average teen-ager nowadays has been reared at three or four addresses.

I have often wondered if a modern city family were given fifty acres in a secluded wilderness or prairie land, along with a gift of a thousand dollars and even the means of getting there, what the result would be. My guess is that to most people, the fifty acres would hold no promise whatsoever except for what price it could be *sold*. And being too far from urban attractions, few city families would have the vision, or courage or even the simple will to pioneer a farm.

...the spires of
the older section
of town...

The Spirit of GODLINESS

A religious regard for nature and the spiritual is an indispensable element of greatness. As man develops and disturbs nature's relationship with the Creator, not only does the quality of the landscape become mediocre but the same loss of character seems to occur to the disturber himself.

It is strange that in an age of scientific greatness, there should be an increasing mediocrity in mankind. One might think that now with so many people and such astounding things for them to do, the Book of Great Americans would be all the more crowded with notable names. As we look backward into the past of politics and art and writing and philosophy, great names stand out: simple names like Johnny Appleseed and Crazy Horse and Miles Standish; powerful names like James Monroe and Benjamin Franklin or Abraham Lincoln or Paul Revere that stir the imagination of youth, like Stephen Vincent Benet's Daniel Boone who "walked by night when phantom deer arise and all lost wild America was burning in their eyes." Today we have to ponder and stretch our minds to name any giants of our time, only to find that most of our great people are really more publicized than deserving.

A great man is one who believes his life belongs to civilization —that whatever God has bestowed upon him, he (in a godlike manner) automatically gives to mankind. As we regard our discordant culture with historic eye and analyze what we call modern art and modern writing and modern politics, there becomes little doubt that there were greater people in America one time than there are today. There were more sincere artists than psychopathic painters, more distinguished statesmen than opportunist politicians, more thinking poets and writers than sensationalists. There were very few old-timers who considered the doctrine that there is health in madness: civilization was based upon godliness.

People are quick to give me argument that the spirit of godliness has vanished or that it has even decreased in America. But the worship of money is so commonplace and engulfing that we are seldom aware of it, or what has happened to church worship in two hundred years. "No people," said George Washington, "can be bound to acknowledge and adore that invisible hand which conducts the affairs of men, more than the people of these United States." At that time, everyone attended services every Sunday and the church was the center of each village. Conducting business on the Sabbath was punishable; toll bridges were free; it was the custom to walk to church if possible rather than upset the decorum of the day with horses and carriages. Generally speaking, church-going in America has decreased from ninety percent to something less than ten percent.

The critics of early American life contend there was too much religion in those Puritan days. Even when you learned your alphabet, the illustrations were all Biblical (A for Adam, B for Bible, C for Christ, and so on). But we should remember that there were no schoolbooks then, and the always present Bible became the major (and often only) textbook. There were no professional teachers, so the preacher of Sunday became schoolteacher all the rest of the week. Without the church there would have been no early American schools.

The church in Washington's time was the main support in American life: today it is more an embellishment. The churchgoer of yesterday sought main support from the church but the churchgoer today merely embellishes his life with his occasional attendance.

Just as religion once tied together the family and surrounded the whole American community, the nation and its government was likewise fathered by the profound belief in God. The national emblem (the Great Seal) is crowned by His eye—we usually have to refer to the dollar bill to refresh our memory of what the Great Seal looks like, or even to recall our national motto, In God We Trust. It was the conviction of the founding fathers, and the frequent words of George Washington, that "to attempt government without God is impossible." Like it or not, accept it or not, the Bible was once the main source of America's national identity.

Villages no longer are born around a central church; instead they start around wherever a bank is built. The smallest shopping mart on the outskirts of any small village may install a bank and only then does it become established as a community. Off the highway nowadays, as you speed past roadside communities, you can occasionally see the tall white spires of early churches still standing in what is known as "the older sections of towns." I called this to the attention of one banker who agreed with me. "Some of the more fervent prayers," he said, "are not said in the church at all, but right here in the bank."

Although the old-time church is declining, there is a new godliness emerging in America: not all Sunday School dropouts have been without the Spirit. Youthful evangelical groups have increased almost as fast as theological denominations have decreased. The very first church-meetings in America were held in the open, in barns or under trees. Perhaps from those new evangelical denominations, from Billy Graham to Jesus Freaks, will evolve something like that kind of primitive American godliness which has been lacking of late; after all, it takes people, not a creed, to make a church. Religion hardly permeates today's scene, but if Christ returned he'd have a more profound audience among those everyday young evangelical groups than he would at eleven o'clock each Sunday at the town church. I think He'd be pleased.

Like Einstein who did not visualize the traditional personal God, twentieth-century America must still admire the structure of the universe as far as it is revealed to our weak powers of recognition. That would be the least demanded by a Creator.

"...the wealth
of America is
her farms."

T. Jefferson

The Spirit of
AGRONOMY

The original spirit of agronomy can never return any more than Park Avenue can grow potatoes the way it did in the 1700s. But a spirit itself is something that doesn't die, and the reverence for the land as an inherent part of man must for our eventual survival continue to be an American heritage.

In 1958 Eisenhower summed up the nation, saying: "We have progressed from an isolated farm economy to a world industrial economy." That "isolated farm economy" happened to be more than an economy; it was our way of life, a personal and national philosophy. In "progressing," the individual has now become a different person in a different nation. If the pioneer could return today he would certainly be impressed by the wonders of scientific change, but he would also be aware that his unique nation was no more.

Because we have become so business-minded, it is difficult for us to realize that the early American farmer seldom was in the business of *selling* farm produce: instead he raised food for his own family and for his own livestock: farming was the classical way of American life. "Those who labor in the earth," said Jefferson, "are the chosen people of God." Washington had said: "Husbandry was the first employment and the most honorable . . . farming is a divine appointment." Washington and Jefferson, like everyone else, lived active farm lives and knew well the religion of farming. Even in the 1800s, when farming began to be a business instead of a personal necessity, the farmer was still regarded as a special man with a special calling. But in the mid-nineteenth century, things changed.

Like much of early Americana, agronomy changed and began its decline during the Civil War period. Young men returned from an unnecessary war too disillusioned to take up where they had left off: they had seen big cities and quick money. Daddy was no longer the "lord of the earth"; he was regarded as an archaic stay-at-home comic character called Rube, with shoddy clothes, rubber boots and chewing on a blade of grass. The farmstead was no longer an estate built up and left to generation after generation; from then on, children would inherit money instead, and capitalism would become as much a personal philosophy as a national economy.

It is interesting to note how youths recently returned from another useless and unnecessary American war, too disillusioned to go back to where they had left off and how some have gone "back to the earth," trying to live—often without their realizing it—exactly as the early Americans did. Unfortunately, this is a small movement, and the cement age is so complete, quick, and powerful that "improved" and "developed" lands can never revert to farms again. Farming is geared only to big business and the spirit of agronomy is a vanished American trait.

Push-button machinery and synthetic manures have pushed agronomy so far from nature that the modern farmer is seldom more than a businessman in overalls or a rural manufacturer. Cattle made overfat usually by (cancer-producing) drugs can hardly walk and sometimes need help to rise from a lying down position; but they do make the tenderest steaks in two hundred years. Some farmers have raised crops with the sole purpose of destroying them and some are paid by the government for not raising them at all; but they are the richest farmers in two hundred years. If the farmer of 1776 could return he would find a very different American way of life.

Whereas the government had a reverence for the farmer two hundred years ago, it now discourages private farming. Because of taxes it is driving thousands of farmers each month from their own land, forcing them to sell to real estate developers. The farmer who dares to leave his land to his son knows that farmland will not be taxed as farmland but instead at whatever price the land would bring as a real estate development: a farmer cannot pay such taxes and is therefore forced to sell the farm. In this manner, American countryside soil that took 25,000 years to develop into fine farmland is bulldozed away and "improved," bringing tax riches to the government but nevertheless impoverishing the nation ecologically.

I have often read about the American Indian's belief that God owns the earth and that man is only a tenant upon it: the idea seems primitive and quaint to us nowadays. Yet the sooner we realize it is a basic truth, the better for civilization. America is proud of its cities and highways, all its developments and improvements, but in the eyes of Whoever or Whatever created the earth and its countryside, we might well hang our heads in shame.

The Spirit of TIME

The fact that there were covered bridges long before the United States of America, and that Washington really didn't cross this or that covered bridge (in fact the first American covered bridge appeared after his time) is discouraging to many. Actually the ancient covered bridge makes a much better monument than it does proper highway equipment, which is also discouraging. It is good to look upon symbols of the American past but 1776 is not 1976, nostalgia is a deceiving trap, and the past is not entirely retrievable.

Nostalgia, it seems, has become a fashionable disease. I use the word *disease* correctly (and interestingly) for according to semantics it is a "dis-ease" or discomfort of the present, which so often invites us to return to a calmer and more meaningful past. Like many maladies, which are involuntary physical escapes of the body, nostalgia is a voluntary escape of the mind. Webster says it is: "a longing for familiar or beloved circumstances which are now remote or irrecoverable." Freud suggests it is: "a wish to return to the womb."

An interesting lesson I have learned from the old covered bridges is the inevitable sign "Walk Your Horses." People were seldom in a hurry then, and they well knew the dangers of haste: of course, galloping horses created a straining rhythm that weakened a wooden bridge. But the art of doing things slowly applied to almost everything they did. Haste was considered vulgar and anyone in a hurry was not considered entirely civilized. Benjamin Franklin said: "Only fraud and deceit are ever in a hurry: take time for all things for great haste makes great waste." Emerson reflected his time when he said: "Manners require time, as nothing is more vulgar than haste."

The slow heartbeat of the early countryside surely must have also produced a slower heartbeat in the early American man for he reflected his surroundings. If you have ever observed an old-timer at his chores on the unmechanized farm, you will be impressed by the slow steady pace; you might mistake it for weariness but his timing is properly set to get the most work done with the least exertion. Reaping in the fields, he may give you the same impression of working in his sleep; but at the end of the day he will have cut more grain and be less tired than the man who works in haste.

The early American made remarkable use of each minute. You will now hear people say when they see the carefully made things done long ago: "Those people had all the time in the world—that is how they came to do such extraordinary work." Actually they had only about a fourth of the time we have. To begin with, their average life span was shorter. Without electricity and machinery, handmade things took longer to create. Without quick travel or even highways, time-savers and electric lights, the workday itself was shorter. No matter what you worked at, because of horse-and-wagon farm existence, the average man did early morning chores of what man would now consider a whole day's worth of hard labor, even before he left for his business. The sands of time two hundred years ago ran about ten times faster than they do now.

I remember when learning to fly how the most experienced pilot was he who made the slowest turns and the smoothest maneuvers: the object of this was not only to make the least strain on the aircraft but also to exhibit grace in flight. Likewise when I drove my Model T Ford, the art of driving was to do it smoothly, without grinding the gears and becoming rough with the engine: now the process has changed. Drag racing, considered a fine art among today's young drivers, is where you can put the most strain on the engine, twist the body hardest, leave the most pounds of hot rubber tires behind, and simply go faster.

A few miles from where I live in Connecticut, a group of young people recently decided to experience the past: they would build a house in the woods, just as it would have been done two centuries ago. Immediately they found there was the weather and the seasons to contend with; trees would have to be felled in the fall when the foliage had fallen, and the stripped trunks would have to be carted away during winter when there was ice and snow to glide them over. A lot of the work had to be done in the evening by moonlight, so the almanac and the calendar with its chart of copious moonlight nights became important. Time and timing, they found, was once more important than it is nowadays: every minute, every hour, and every week had its own special use. Each day became a miniature eternity. The work seemed slower but, after two years of labor, there was a house stronger than anything else in the neighborhood and it housed people who knew there can be more real life in the countryman's day than there can be in a whole year for the average city businessman.

Although people used to have a righteous contempt for anything done in a rush, speed has become today's fullest measure of efficiency. Time-savers are an obsession, but the time saved is only squandered; it is like hoarding money in order to be extravagant. "Dost thou love life?" asked Benjamin Franklin two centuries ago. "Then do not squander *time,* for that is what *life* is made of."

Time seems to have become only waste material, and according to modern reasoning, only the successful or rich man can afford the luxury of wasting it. Retiring has become an American sign of affluence and the new philosophy is to work hard and make your money quickly so you can retire earlier. There is no doubt about it, the spirit of time and timing has changed.

We have become artists at the business of going fast, but going slowly is an equally important art which should not be ignored. We have made giant strides in our time yet Franklin's words come prophetically from a distant past: "Haste makes waste," and ecologically speaking, are words of global wisdom. "Walk your horses" is no more than quaint nostalgia, but youth has a more timely advice: "Take it easy—you'll last longer."

51

"... an astounding
Independence"

the Spirit of
INDEPENDENCE

"You may well understand the Declaration of Independence," read one letter from a European traveling through the New World in 1810, "when you see the great stone barns of Pennsylvania. The American farmer lives like a baron in a land of plenty and with an astounding independence."

I remember when doing a book about early American barns that I described such buildings as being *unique;* and how the architectural experts took me to task at once, declaring that similar structures (even better and bigger) had been built in many places abroad. I suppose I was being poetic and subtle for I was not thinking of four walls and a roof but instead was regarding the barn aesthetically, why it was built and how it was being used. The early European barns had always been built by the landlords, the king, or for the church as savings banks for peasant tithes and taxes in the form of hay and grain. The lowly farmer himself had nothing but a rough shack or shelter for his tools and a horse or two. Only in America did he become independent and build a completely independent barn, often ten times larger than his dwelling. With emotions of joy and pride and thankfulness, he copied the giant tithe barns of overseas, making the early American barn an agricultural challenge to fill. The walls and roof may have looked the same but the aura of American thinking made the barn new, different, unique. As a finishing touch almost in ridicule of European crests and church markings, the farmer added his own decoration—not a hex sign as many now call it—and the giant American barn was born.

I have done a lot of writing about the early American but I shall be the first to admit that except for the Indian there were actually no such human beings as early Americans. The Dutch and German and English and French became American when they became independent and "thought American." Thoreau was thinking American when he said he would rather sit on a pumpkin and have it all to himself than be crowded on a velvet cushion: Emerson was voicing the same philosophy of independence when he said every man is unique.

Everyone knows about "the American heritage" but, when asked, few can say what that heritage is. Boiled down to a sentence, what made us different, what tilted Europe off her moral base and created the foundation for a United States of America was independence and *total respect for the individual*. The Declaration of Independence stated that the greatest human benefit is independence—that independence shall be the American way and the American heritage.

The power of independence and the strength of individualism was more alive and evident when the nation was young, when everyone was more aware of their newfound credo but nowadays we are so stuffed with science and "better living" that we take independence for granted. The national birthday used to be called Independence Day and it was both solemn and joyous with prayers and speeches and celebration: bells started ringing at midnight on the third of July and continued throughout the day. It was during the Civil War period that Independence Day bell-ringing was forgotten when gunfire and fireworks took over. Now the great day is called "The Fourth of July" and copying George Washington's birthday, the stores feature special sales to celebrate it.

Independence and individuality do not take indifference lightly; they start to decay when they are ignored, and today is an era of indifference. Apathy is an invincible and insidious giant. It dares to make the great American dream a self-induced slumber. Already mass-produced machinery has created a mass-produced civilization in which the individual often has less importance than the machine. Individualism is in a twilight of its favor: mediocrity finds both safety and acceptance in standardization. Management has become computerized, mechanical, and conformist while workers are willingly compelled to let unions do their thinking. The man with a mind of his own is regarded as a radical. Never has American individualism and independence been so lacking: its power cries for rebirth and the independent man's moral strength to speak out.

The bicentennial of the United States could be a vulgar display of wealth and accomplishment; better a greater revival of what it was two hundred years ago—a *celebration* of *independence*. Americans at that time started that day in church, but there is a small chance of reviving that custom. People used to carry flags then without being "suspect" or "reactionary." There are birthday greetings and cards for every known holiday but the only Independence Day cards I have seen are those in my collection of American antiques.

I have been criticized for naming this writing *The Spirits of '76*. The word "spirits," they argued, sounds too much like "ghosts" or "liquor." That, to me, is a commentary on these times when moral spirits are so lagging. I have an early sampler done by a thirteen-year-old girl. On it is a thought that pertains as much to the nation as it does to the individual:

He that loses wealth loseth much; he that loseth friends loseth more; but he that loseth spirit loseth all.

May God bless and revive in this country the spirits of '76.

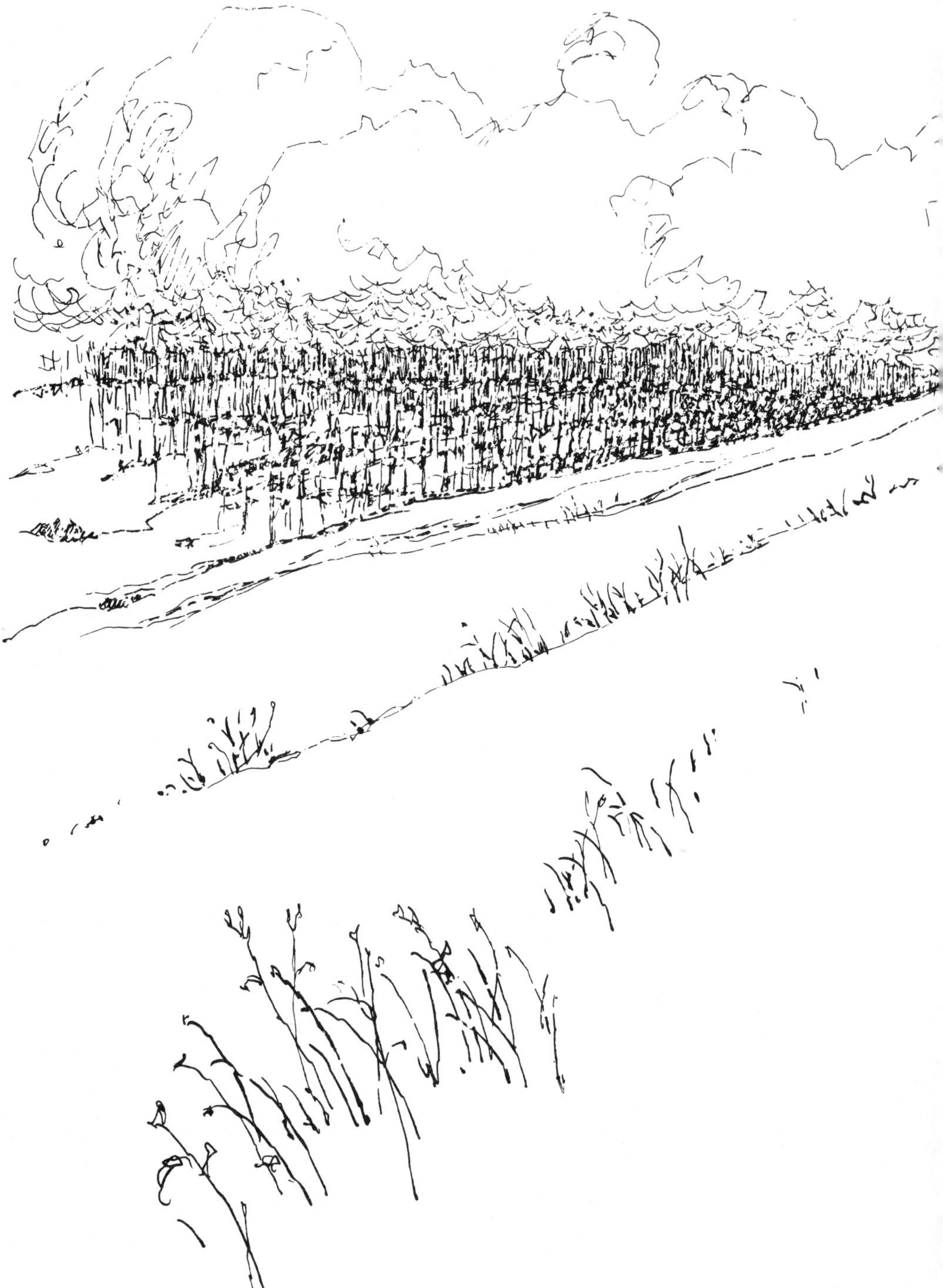

The Spirit of AWARENESS

I once spent a Vermont winter snowed into seclusion. It was before television but I had a store of wood and books and food. I thought life would be dull yet I found myself rising at dawn to put in a full day of writing and painting and enjoying the extraordinary phenomenon of life. The intense awareness of existence produced by solitude can be a thrilling delight; I doubt it is possible to experience today. I don't live in the city now, but as I type these words I can hear my furnace at work; my telephone rings every few minutes; I automatically switch the radio on for news every hour; my typewriter drums a tune and rings a bell to add to the symphony of a thousand tiny distractions; I must hurry because I have a dinner reservation within the hour. My remembered winter in Vermont is like a dream from a distant world, but profound awareness is still with me, alive and reassuring.

Few writers knew New England as did Van Wyck Brooks. When first I moved to his Connecticut I told him that I found the countryside lonely. "But I enjoy it," I added. "That," he declared, "makes you an old school American." He had already written about that. "Loneliness," he wrote, "is stamped on the American face; it rises like an exhalation from the American landscape."

At one time loneliness was a creditable American quality but now even the word has changed—it has become a distasteful state with a dictionary definition that includes "sadness" and "desolate." A century ago, however, the word meant: "the love of retirement; a disposition toward solitude and seclusion." I might add that loneliness was also the key to exquisite awareness, lacking in the mechanized carousel of confusion that is today.

Thomas Wolfe accepted loneliness. "The whole conviction of my life," he wrote, "now rests upon the belief that loneliness, far from being a rare and curious phenomenon peculiar to myself and to a few other solitary men, is the central and inevitable fact of human existence." The loneliness of modern man is a strange paradox for the richer he becomes and the more crowded his life, the lonelier he may become. Within the last few decades, the lonely American has found solace and refuge by becoming a collector. He might argue a passion for history, the wisdom of collecting precious metals or the hobby of keeping commemorative medals and plates; but beneath the popular vogue is the fact that the collector is usually a man seeking awareness and recognition—a lonely person who has found a key to importance and escape from loneliness.

In 1955 I wrote a book called *American Yesterday* in which I tried to compare the man of yesterday with the man of today. I suppose it started the trend of thought which ended in this book. But I found that the most important difference between the early American and his modern counterpart, if boiled down to one word, was *awareness*. The early life was saturated with the essence of awareness that made living a vital experience; today we exist in a dreamlike life where everything it done for us and we seem to have very little part in the play of our own destiny. The living oblivion of apathy produces twentieth-century mediocrity.

I remember hosting a New Mexican Indian friend from the Taos reservation, showing him the wonders of New York City and its skyscrapers for the first time. Of course, I was most interested in what his impressions would be. "What impresses me most," he told me, "are the people. They all look as if they are walking and running in their sleep. They have no faces."

He was right: you see them now, sitting in buses, at plays and in subways, in elevators and at restaurants, working in offices or at bars, walking along the streets withdrawn from the world, hiding behind blank masks. In the country still, or a century ago, people nodded, smiled, or spoke; now city people are victims of automation, congestion, affluence, self-protection, and lack of purpose, with the immense sadness of unawareness.

The conglomeration of man-made distractions in modern life, the explosions of light and sound that gyrate into a kaleidoscopic maze, is hypnotic. A sharp word or a kind remark, a strain of song or any bit of ordinary human emotion can break the trance. I remember seeing a girl walking down Fifth Avenue with a glowing smile on her face; she looked straight ahead but everyone turned to stare. Where contentment is rare, a simple human expression had broken through the mechanical texture of city existence.

Living two centuries ago was a more conscious experience because each thing we did was done to its fullest, which made us more aware of living. Drinking water used to be tasting your own water from a well that you dug yourself; now you turn a faucet and water appears in a mysterious manner from some unknown place. Illuminating a room was lighting candles that you had created yourself; now you turn on a switch and light arrives from a mysterious power from God knows where (often the power company itself is not certain). Eating used to be tasting food that you grew and raised yourself, then cooked at home; now we seldom know what we are eating or where it comes from. This morning I decided to learn what my cold breakfast drink really was, so I read the label: it was cellulose gum, potassium citrate, citric acid, calcium phosphate, hydrogenated coconut oil, preservative BHA, and artificial flavor. The rest was plain sugar and water. It was what the astronauts had for breakfast in space, but forgive me for being an old-fashioned person who likes oranges the way my God made them.

The extent of unawareness today would be unbelievable to the early American. All the necessities of life being made for you or done for you by someone unknown from somewhere unknown, produces a dehumanized existence in which the only part left for us to play is to pay out money in exchange. The old-timer seldom paid out money; instead he knew the source, the ingredients, and results of his everyday life; this gave him the satisfaction of self-security and self-vitality instead of existing in a somnambulistic state as modern man tends to do. Recently there has been a faddish escape to our nation's past which we choose to call nostalgia: when mankind loses vitality he looks for it in his past, and enjoys play-acting what he has already lost. David Lillienthal said, "The well-springs of our vitality are not economic; they go deeper still—they are ethical and spiritual."

One of the charms of early American artifacts is that the maker nearly always signed his name or initials and the date it was done. We now regard this as a quaint custom, but it was really a key to the spirit of awareness that permeated those profound times. Men were conscious of their position in the new nation and they did not want to be anonymous: when you create for posterity you are most apt to be excellent and then make proper record of your creation.

John Adams wrote: "Posterity! you will never know how much it cost the present generation to preserve your freedom!" He was right; we are not aware, and so often we care less. Unawareness is a weakness but indifference is a sickness. Moral indifference, that malady of the cultivated classes, is more of a national danger than any foreign threat, and the antidote is awareness.

As wealth and affluence are not the lifeblood of man, neither are they the lifeblood of a nation. The real reason for being is the awareness and pursuit of purpose. The statement of purpose written in 1776 created the lifeblood and heritage of the American dream: to be aware of that purpose is important—the end comes with unawareness.

The SPIRITS of '76

"...*if cut down, it will
                sprout again.*"

HOPE...

When the preceding manuscript was left on my secretary's desk to be typed into more readable form, it was accompanied by my usual author's request: "Please let me know your reactions to this writing."

When the manuscript was typed, I found a note attached: "This is an interesting and moving piece of writing but it is sad in its implications. It doesn't leave much hope."

I was grateful for that comment, which urged me to add this postscript—an eleventh American spirit that fortunately has not vanished from the scene, the spirit of *hope*. I suppose there has been pessimism in my nostalgia and like Benjamin Franklin I have been reasoning that: "He who lives on hope alone will die fasting." But I find more lasting logic in the Bible's: "There is hope of a tree, if cut down, that it will sprout again" (Job, X 14:9). After all, a spirit is that which has no death and the old spirits of America can still sprout up again sometime, somewhere. Once you *know* them, even as small voices from far away, they will surely endure even the loud bombardment of modern change.

Perhaps the pollution of affluence, congestion, automation, money, and lack of purpose, which has in two hundred years managed to foul up the national machine, needs a new filter. The young have new, clean, strong filters that can screen out the good from the bad more quickly than we older worn-out people: in youth lies hope. I am convinced that the spiritual pollution, which has changed so thoroughly moral a nation, is not as strong as the powerful spirits it was born with; that in living for Today, we can dream for Tomorrow and learn from Yesterday.